BEING
BLIND

Peter White

Chrysalis Children's Books

First published in the UK in 1998 by
(i) Chrysalis Children's Books
An imprint of Chrysalis Books Group PLC
The Chrysalis Building, Bramley Road, London W10 6SP

Paperback edition first published in 2004

ISBN 1 85561 796 X (hb)
ISBN 1 84138 789 4 (pb)
British Library Cataloguing in Publication Data for this book
is available from the British Library.

Printed in Hong Kong
10 9 8 7 6 5 4 3 2 (hb)
10 9 8 7 6 5 4 3 2 1 (pb)

Editor: Stephanie Bellwood
Designer: Guy Callaby
Picture researcher: Diana Morris
Illustrator: Richard Prideaux
Consultants: Bernard Fleming, Royal National Institute for the Blind
                Elizabeth Atkinson
With thanks to Professor Elkington, Eye Unit, Southampton General Hospital

Picture acknowledgements:
Baum Elektronik: 28bl. BBC Photographs: 3. Bridgeman Art Library: 9c Bibliothèque
Nationale, Paris. Brytech Inc: 8tl. Christian Blind Mission: 7t. Clearvision: 13tr. Collections:
front cover & 16t Anthea Sieveking, 18t Brian Shuel, 28r Lesley Howling. Dee Conway: 21b.
DfEE: 27b. Mary Evans Picture Library: 8b. Eye Ubiquitous: 19t Paul Seheult. Getty Images:
4b Andrea Booher, 5t Tony Latham, 6t Ken Fisher, 8tr Art Brewer, 10b UHB Trust, 14t
Arthur Tilley, 20t Alan Levenson, 22t Frank Ores, 24 Tony Latham, 26b, 28t Penny Gentieu.
Sally & Richard Greenhill: 23c. The Guide Dogs for the Blind Association: 17tr. Rebecca
Harris: 21. Image Bank: 10t Jane Art. Imperial War Museum, London: 16b. London
Metropolitan Archives: 9t, 14b. The Nottingham Group Ltd: 12b. Redferns: 27t David
Refern. Retrograph Archive: 26c. RNIB: 5b, 6b Isabel Lilly, 17tl Bob Kauders, 18b, 19c, 22b,
23t, 25t, 25c. Royal London Society for the Blind: 11ct, 11cb, 11b, 15b all Eric Richmond.
Spectrum Colour Library: 20b. SPL: 11t Will & Deni McIntyre, 13tl Adam Hart Davis, 28b
Hank Morgan. Stockmarket/Zefa: 4t K & H Benser, 12t, 26t.

Words in **bold** are explained in the glossary on pages 30 and 31.

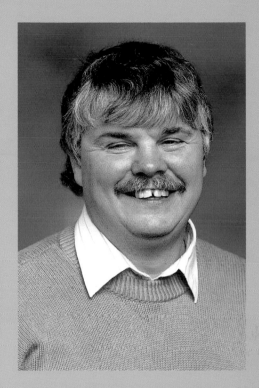

Contents

ABOUT THE AUTHOR

Peter White has been blind all his life. His older brother is also blind. Being blind did not stop Peter from becoming a journalist, writer and broadcaster.

Peter is the BBC Disability Affairs Correspondent. He provides information for television and radio programmes whenever they need an expert on disability issues.

For over 20 years Peter has presented a radio programme for blind and partially-sighted people called *In Touch*. He has worked on television programmes for disabled people, such as *Link* on ITV and *Same Difference* on Channel 4. He often writes for journals and magazines.

Peter is married with four children. He travels to London every day to work at the BBC.

Understanding blindness

Have you ever played games where you wore a blindfold? You probably stumbled around, bumping into tables, walls and other people! If you watch a blind person, you'll notice that they have much more control. They quickly remember where familiar things are, and they learn to be aware of objects around them.

Levels of blindness

Only one in every five blind people can see nothing at all. Most blind people have some vision, even if it is only shadowy. They learn to use their limited vision and other senses so skilfully that you might not realize how little they can see.

The right hand side of this photograph shows how the world looks to many people with damaged sight. This is a common form of blindness.

Everyday activities

What everyday things would be difficult if you couldn't see? How would you find your clothes and get dressed in the morning? You would need to be very organized. Blind people keep their clothes in separate drawers or in a certain order so they know exactly where everything is. Some totally blind people use their sense of touch to recognize things.

The sense of touch can be very useful to people who can see nothing at all.

THINK ABOUT

Meal time

If you were blind how would you know what you were eating before you put it into your mouth? People with no sight at all use smell and touch to guess what's on the plate. Some people use the clock method. They imagine their plate is a clock and are told that pizza is at five o'clock, peas are at eight o'clock, and so on. Or sometimes they just stick a fork in and hope for the best!

Keeping up with technology

It's not true that all blind people miss out on things like television. You'd be surprised how much they can work out by listening carefully and using their limited sight and a bit of imagination. Computers can be **adapted** for blind people by having large print. Some computers speak or have a **Braille** printer. This **partially-sighted** boy can see the bright shapes on the screen.

What is blindness?

A few people can see nothing at all, but most of the people we call blind can see a little. People with poor vision are called **partially-sighted**. Many people are **short-sighted** or **long-sighted**. Most kinds of blindness are more likely to affect people as they grow old, but a disease or an accident can harm eyes at any time. Now and then children are born blind or with very poor sight.

A human eye

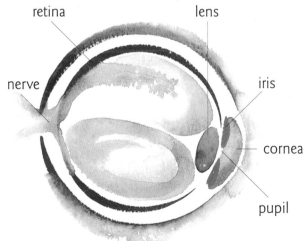

retina

lens

nerve

iris

cornea

pupil

How the eye works

The eye is like a camera. It takes a picture through the **lens** just like a camera does. The back of the eye is like the film where the photograph is stored. **Nerve** messages carry the picture to the brain. Any part of the eye can go wrong. This is why there are so many different kinds of blindness.

Why do people go blind?

Cataracts are one of the most common causes of blindness. They usually affect adults but children can have them too. Cataracts grow in the lens of the eye and make people feel as if they are looking through clouds. Part of the **retina** can also be damaged. This stops the person from seeing detail. Some people have a disease called **glaucoma**.

A boy at a school for blind children practises his handwriting. He makes the letters big so that he can see them see better.

Dangerous diseases

Illnesses such as **diabetes** and **AIDS** can affect many parts of the body including the eyes. A lot of people in the world's poorer countries are blinded by diseases. In parts of Africa a disease called river blindness is carried by a fly that lives near rivers. River blindness can cause whole villages of people to go blind.

This man has river blindness. A child acts as his eyes by leading him along. Many people in poor countries cannot afford an operation to save their sight.

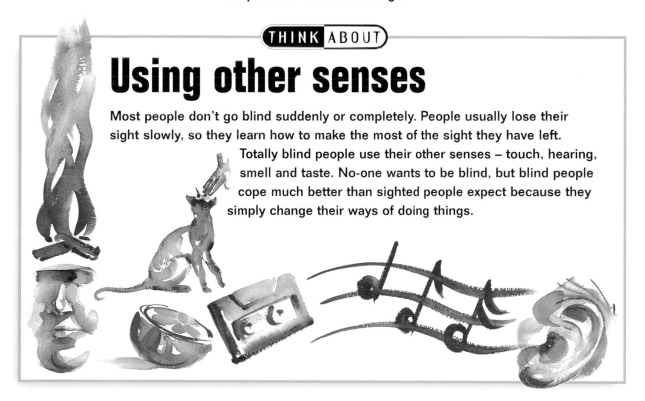

THINK ABOUT

Using other senses

Most people don't go blind suddenly or completely. People usually lose their sight slowly, so they learn how to make the most of the sight they have left.

Totally blind people use their other senses – touch, hearing, smell and taste. No-one wants to be blind, but blind people cope much better than sighted people expect because they simply change their ways of doing things.

Blindness over the years

Blindness has often puzzled people, and sometimes it has frightened them too. Warriors such as the Spartans from ancient Greece thought that blind people were no use because they could not fight. Babies who were born blind were left outside to die. Other people, such as the Romans, believed that blind people had special powers and that they could see into the future.

Treatment for blindness

A hundred years ago people didn't know much about eyes and what could go wrong with them, and they often believed that blindness was a punishment for people who had behaved badly. People who went blind were tricked into thinking that powders and potions would cure their blindness, when really they did no good at all.

▶ Eye operations were painful and messy in the years before modern surgery. This drawing shows an eye operation in eighteenth-century France.

Learning and working

Most blind children were not educated, and they had to stay at home instead of going to school. Until the invention of the **Braille** system in 1824 they had no way of reading. Children who did go to school had to try and memorize their lessons. There was not much chance of getting a job, and many blind people had to beg in the street.

Blind people were sometimes given jobs making baskets and brushes. This photograph of girls learning to be basketmakers was taken in the early twentieth century.

This sixteenth-century drawing is one of the first pictures of someone wearing spectacles. Can you spot the monk with the glasses?

A great invention

Nowadays many people wear glasses, but for a long time only a few people were lucky enough to own a pair. No-one knows who thought up the idea for glasses, but we do know that spectacles were first worn in Europe in the thirteenth century.

Help for blindness

Every now and again you may see dramatic stories on the news about blind people suddenly getting back their sight. It sounds exciting but in fact it doesn't happen very often. It's true that doctors have become much better at stopping people's sight getting any worse. They can also help people to make the most of the vision they have left.

What can we put right?
There are ways of helping people with poor sight. Many people wear glasses or contact lenses. Nowadays **cataracts** can be removed with an operation.

Another way of solving eye problems is by taking eye drops that contain useful drugs. Drops get rid of the liquid that can build up behind the eye and make it hurt. They also clear up infections that can make the eye red and sore.

▶ Contact lenses are usually made from a type of plastic. The lens is placed carefully on the surface of the eye. People who wear contact lenses have to clean them every day.

Laser treatment

The **retina** is a sensitive part of the eye, and it can tear. **Laser** treatment can be used to help this. A strong beam of light is directed into the eye and on to the damaged area. The laser joins the small tears with its powerful beam. Laser treatment can also help scars on the eye caused by **diabetes**. It doesn't cure the damaged parts, but it can stop the scars from becoming worse.

Sensory rooms

The world can be a frightening and mysterious place for **partially-sighted** children. Some children enjoy visiting a sensory room with relaxing music to listen to and bright, colourful lights to look at. This helps them to use their sight better.

▲ Laser surgery can be used to help people who are short-sighted or long-sighted.

▶ This partially-sighted boy is able to see lots of colours and shapes in a sensory room.

THINK ABOUT

Helping yourself

Even if their sight can't be improved people find ways of making the best of what they have left. Strong **magnifiers** help people to read, get around, or recognise friends. Sometimes people have to hold their heads in strange-looking positions to help them to see better, and children can make fun of this. If you know someone like this who is being teased you should remember that they are only trying to make the most of their sight.

At home

If you had a blind brother or sister, what kinds of things do you think they would be able to do? Which games would you play with them? How would they make themselves a drink or a piece of toast? As long as a blind child has the right help he or she can join in almost anything that families do together.

Playing games

Many board games can be **adapted** for blind children to play by touch. There are balls with bells or bleepers inside so that they can be heard as well as seen. And there are always games that don't need any equipment, such as hide and seek or truth or dare.

Story time

Blind children have lots of books to chose from. There are large print books, books on tape, **Braille** books and even Braille comics. Some books have raised, bumpy pictures so that blind readers can feel what the characters in the story are like.

▶ **This blind boy and his sighted sister can read together because their book is in Braille and ordinary print as well.**

▲ A blind girl peels potatoes for a meal, using her sense of touch. The more she practises, the easier the task will become.

In the kitchen

When blind people do everyday tasks they use their other senses to make up for not having sight. If they are pouring a drink they listen as the juice goes into the glass, or they simply stick their fingers in the top until something wet touches them. When they cut bread or spread butter they can use their spare hand to check that the knife is straight. And blind people easily learn to work the controls on equipment such as toasters.

THINK ABOUT

Joining in

Blind children have just the same interests as you. They enjoy listening to music, videos and television programmes, and of course just messing about. And as long as you give them a helping hand outside they will be able to go wherever you and your friends go.

At school

Have you ever thought how much of your school work depends on eyesight? You read books, look at computer screens, or watch your teacher doing an experiment. How do you think blind and **partially-sighted** children do the same kind of work?

Special schools

For a long time people thought that the best way to teach blind children was to put them all together in special schools. The schools had equipment such as **Braille** books, writing machines and maps with raised lines. The teachers were all trained to help blind children.

These days more and more blind children go to their local schools and learn with their sighted friends. There are still some very good special schools, but most people now think that blind and sighted children should grow up together wherever possible so that they can learn from each other.

▶ A geography lesson in a school for blind children in 1908. Do you think it was a good idea to keep blind children apart from sighted children by sending them to separate schools?

The Braille system

Braille is a system of raised dots that are combined to form all the letters of the alphabet, as well as punctuation such as commas and full stops. Braille was invented more than 150 years ago. It opened up the world of reading and writing to blind children. Braille is used in books, but it is also used to make maps and diagrams for people to read by touch.

Some blind people learn to read Braille very fast. You need a good sense of touch to feel the bumps.

This girl is learning to use a Braille typewriter in a special centre for young blind children.

THINK ABOUT

Computers

Children with a sight loss can use computers to work and play on just like you. Some computers print extra large letters or have a Braille display. Some computers can even read out what's on the screen. This means that blind children can read what everyone else is reading. They can also write their own projects for others to read. Blind children can be part of the class instead of working on their own.

Reading and writing

There are many ways to make school work easier for blind children. Some children use special writing machines. They look like typewriters and they punch out Braille dots on to thick paper. Children with some sight have books with extra large print. They can also use **magnifiers** to make the print stand out more clearly. Blind children sometimes listen to books and lessons on tape.

Getting around

If you have ever been roller skating in the park you will know that you must think quickly and take notice of the people and objects around you. Blind people rely on the same skills of awareness to get around safely. They use their common sense to work out where they are and what's going on around them. This way they avoid accidents.

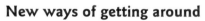

New ways of getting around

In the past blind people found it very difficult to move around independently. It was only after the First World War that doctors began to think about ways to help people who could not see. This was because many soldiers had been blinded in fighting. They were still young and they wanted to work and lead a normal life after the war. The two most successful ideas developed were the **cane** and the **guide dog**.

▶ **These British soldiers were blinded by poison gas in the First World War. Gas was a very dangerous weapon.**

The white cane

Canes were invented after the First World War. People with poor sight had always used sticks to lean on, but canes helped them to avoid obstacles. The canes were made of light metal and coloured white so that they could be seen easily. Many blind people now use a white cane.

Guide dogs for the blind

Another good idea for helping blinded soldiers was to use dogs to lead them. It became so popular that soon blind people all over the world had guide dogs. A dog and its owner are trained to work together. The blind person has to be in control and the dog must know exactly what to do.

A blind boy learns to use a long cane. The cane's red bands show that the boy is deaf too.

THINK ABOUT

Finding the way

Imagine what it would be like to walk to school if you couldn't see. Could you work out which way to go? How would you know when it was safe to cross the road? There is so much traffic on the roads that blind people need a lot of skill and confidence to go out alone. They listen carefully to the sounds around them. They remember which way to turn, and they always cross the road at pedestrian crossings.

Out and about

The outside world is noisy and fast moving. Sighted people just look at signs to find out which shop is which or where the station is. How do you think a blind person can tell which bus to catch, or when they've reached the library or the supermarket?

Listening and remembering

Blind people have always found ways of moving around without much help. Some people work out a lot from the **echo** of their feet on the pavement, and learn to sense when they have reached a road junction or if they are near an obstacle such as a lamp post or bus shelter. Landmarks such as a set of railings or a low wall can help a blind person to remember a route and to check they are going the right way.

◀ **A blind woman finds her way around a busy market. She has a long cane to help her, but her sense of direction is very important as well.**

Crossing the road

There are many new ideas to help blind people. Pedestrian crossings often have sound bleepers that let people know when to cross. Pavements next to the crossing are often bumpy or rough to tell blind people that it's a safe place to cross.

Travelling around

If a blind person wants to know which bus or train has arrived often the best way is to ask other passengers. Clear and detailed announcements help too. In the future there may be talking bus stops, shops, phone boxes and ticket machines that are **programmed** to tell blind people important information.

▲ Have you ever seen Braille signs in public places? This postbox in France has Braille labels.

◀ The inside of this college for blind students has been carefully designed. It is brightly coloured with tall windows to let in lots of light. Handrails along each wall help to guide people.

Inside buildings

There are many things which can be done to help that do not cost a lot of money. Architects could think more about **acoustics** in their buildings so that there aren't too many confusing echoes. Good lighting helps people who have some vision, and clear **contrasting** colours can make it easier for them to see the difference between the walls and the floor.

(THINK ABOUT)

Lending a hand

Even with all these new ideas, there are still many times when you can give blind people a helping hand. It's usually best to let a blind person take your arm while you walk slightly ahead. Guide them carefully past obstacles. The golden rule is always to ask first if help is needed and then check how the blind person wants you to help them. They will know best what makes them feel comfortable.

Fun and games

Blind people enjoy sports and games just as much as sighted people. They find ways of **adapting** sports to make them easier. For example, they play ball games by putting a bell or something that rattles inside the ball. You might think that a blind person couldn't ride a bicycle, but what about riding a tandem with a sighted person in front?

All sorts of sport

Some sports are easier for blind people than you might think. Swimming can be good fun for someone who is totally blind because they are in an enclosed area. There is also a wall around the pool that helps them steer themselves. And if you enjoy swimming you will know that sight is not really important, because when you swim very fast you have your head under the water most of the time. There are also blind athletes. They take part in races by running alongside a sighted guide or having a 'caller' at the end of the track who shouts out instructions.

Being blind does not stop some people being good athletes. This runner has a sighted guide who makes sure that he stays inside his lane.

Art and craft

You don't have to have good eyesight to be an artist. Many blind people enjoy all sorts of arts and crafts. Some people who can't see enough to paint try pottery-making or sculpture instead.

Sport and hobbies

Think about the things you enjoy doing then work out how a blind person might join in. Could they ride a horse or sail a boat? What kind of holiday might they enjoy? Can you think of anything a blind person couldn't do? It's harder than you think.

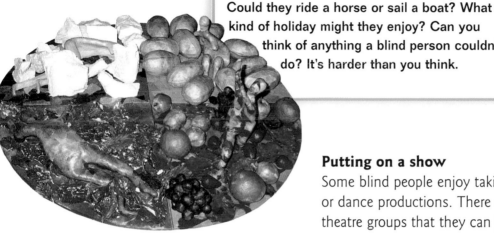

This colourful sculpture is by a blind artist called Rebecca Harris. She made it using papier-mâché, clay, polystyrene and tissue paper.

Putting on a show

Some blind people enjoy taking part in drama or dance productions. There are many blind theatre groups that they can join. Blind actors learn their way around the stage in the same way as they memorize the route to the shops or the way around their house.

In this dance production, the dressed-up man in the middle is a blind actor. The other actors guided him around the stage, but they did it so cleverly that the audience didn't notice.

Going to work

Just like sighted people, blind people want a job when they grow up. They often have the right skills, but many employers are afraid that a blind person won't be able to do the job properly. This is why only about one in four blind people of working age in Britain and the United States has a job.

Working in radio

Roger Smith is a DJ with his own radio show. He works on a radio station at a college for blind people. He was determined that being blind would not stop him doing a job he enjoys.

Roger knows exactly where everything is in the studio, so he has no problems doing live radio shows.

Using computers

In the past people thought that blind people couldn't do complicated or difficult jobs. Nowadays blind people take on all kinds of different jobs. Computers have helped a lot. They allow blind people to read reports and to write their own.

Training to be a pilot

Ken Woodward was blinded in an accident a few years ago. Now he has a job in an office and has also trained as a pilot. He uses his other senses to help him fly, and he listens carefully to the instructions his co-pilot gives him through the headset.

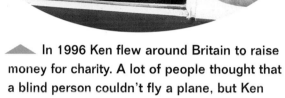 In 1996 Ken flew around Britain to raise money for charity. A lot of people thought that a blind person couldn't fly a plane, but Ken proved them wrong.

This guide dog has been trained to help its owner to work safely. You must never distract guide dogs by feeding, patting or talking to them.

Being in charge

It takes a lot of confidence and skill to run a company. This blind woman has her own computer business. She travels to work every morning with the help of her guide dog.

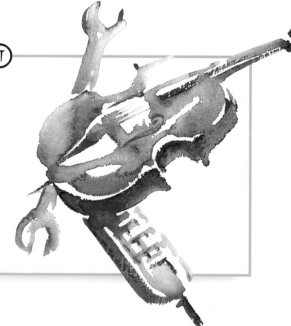

(THINK ABOUT)

Careers

Think about a job you would like to do. Could a blind person do it? Maybe they couldn't drive a taxi, but what about operating the radio to tell drivers where to go? They might not be able to play football, but what about looking after players who are injured and helping them work out their training programme? Blind people can do all kinds of jobs if they are given the chance.

Amazing inventions

Scientists, inventors and ordinary people are always thinking of ideas to help blind people. Some of their inventions are very expensive, such as computers that talk and machines that read and write. Some inventions are simple and cheap, such as putting different shaped buttons on a shirt or a dress to tell you what colour it is.

Pouring a drink

One man thought of a good idea when his father became blind. He noticed that his father had trouble pouring a cup of tea, so he invented a **gadget** that hangs on the edge of a cup and makes a bleeping noise when the hot liquid reaches the top.

Pouring boiling water could be very dangerous without one of these gadgets. They are brightly coloured so that partially-sighted people can see them better.

Telling the time

Everyone needs to be able to tell the time. **Tactile** watches are designed to help blind people tell the time by touch. There are also watches that speak or have extra big numbers.

The lid of this tactile watch lifts up so that a blind person can feel the hands and the bumps next to each number.

Hundreds of inventions

Many ordinary objects are **adapted** for blind people to use. Bathroom scales, microwave ovens and thermometers have all been designed to speak. There are all kinds of helpful gadgets for the kitchen, such as measuring jugs with raised markings, and a metal disc that is placed in the bottom of a pan and rattles when the liquid boils.

This telephone has very large buttons so that people who are partially-sighted can see which numbers to dial.

THINK ABOUT

New ideas

Think of ways to redesign your favourite games so that a blind friend could play them with you. What would need to be changed? Perhaps the board and the pieces could be bigger. Maybe the dots on dominoes could be raised or the snakes and ladders on a board could be bumpy so that you could feel them. How about replacing coloured counters with shapes or changing fiddly flat counters to pegs that fit in holes?

Being a success

Most people think that it must be difficult for blind people to lead a normal life. They often don't realize how much people without sight can do. This means that blind people have to work very hard to persuade others to give them chances. But through history there have been many blind people who achieved great things.

Louis Braille (1809-1852)

Louis Braille lost his sight in an accident at the age of three. He invented the **Braille** system when he was 15 years old, but because he was blind and only a child, no-one took much notice. It was only after his death that people realized how brilliant his idea was.

▲ In this advertisement Louis Braille is remembered as a great man who gave blind people the chance to read.

Helen Keller (1880-1968)

Helen Keller became blind and deaf at the age of two after suffering from **German measles**. At first she could not communicate at all, but with a lot of patience she learned to speak and to read Braille. She became a great writer and teacher, and gave talks all over the world to raise money for deaf and blind people.

◀ Helen Keller discovered that she could tell what someone was saying by feeling their faces and lips as they spoke. This isn't something that blind people normally do, but for Helen Keller it was the only way to share a conversation.

Stevie Wonder (born 1950)

Stevie Wonder is one of the world's most famous musicians. He has been blind since he was born. He made his first record when he was ten years old, and since then he has written and performed music all over the world. He sings and also plays the harmonica, the piano, the organ and the drums.

David Blunkett (born 1947)

The man who runs all the schools in Britain is blind. His name is David Blunkett. He went to a school for blind children in Sheffield and later he became the leader of Sheffield City Council. He is now a leading politician in the British government and he and his **guide dog** are often seen on television.

Stevie Wonder in concert. He often helps to raise money for other blind people.

David Blunkett MP and his guide dog Lucy, who stays with him all day at work.

THINK ABOUT

Fame

Have you heard of any other famous blind people? Try and find out about more blind achievers. Think about the problems they had and how they overcame them.

Looking to the future

One hundred years ago many blind children didn't go to school and not many of them found jobs. There were only a few **Braille** books, no **guide dogs** and those who dared to go out held on to someone's arm or leaned on a stick. A lot has changed over the past hundred years. So what can we expect from the next hundred?

Improving eyesight

Blindness will probably never disappear altogether, but treatment for eye problems is improving all the time. There are some exciting new ideas such as a **bionic** eye that will **transmit** what we see straight to the brain, missing out the part of the eye or the **nerve** that is damaged. But this may be a long way off, or perhaps not possible at all.

Mobility aids

Some blind people now use special **laser** and **radar** equipment to help them move around. These devices are held or worn like glasses, and they give out sound messages about obstacles in front of the person. A machine that acts as a mechanical guide dog is also being developed. It will tell the blind person where obstacles are and then guide the person round them.

Many people are now developing aids for getting around. But do you think many blind people would want to carry all this equipment?

This headband is part of a device called a Sonic Pathfinder. It gives out signals to tell the blind person if there is an object in front of them. It can't guide the person, so they would need to use a guide dog or a long cane as well.

Computerized help

More blind and sighted people have computers at home than ever before. People can do the shopping, get books from the library, or even do school courses without having to leave the house. The Internet allows people to find out all kinds of information. In the next few years both blind and sighted people will be able to do even more using computers.

Many blind children enjoy reading stories or looking at pictures on computer. The print is extra big and sometimes the pictures move too.

THINK ABOUT

Ways to help

Everyone can do their bit to help blind people. It just takes a bit of imagination. It would help blind people if notices were written in Braille or put on tape, or if people didn't leave bicycles and cars on pavements. People should remember that being blind just means that someone can't see, not that they can't think! Inventors and scientists help blind people a lot, but families and friends can do even more.

Glossary

acoustics How sound is heard. In a building with bad acoustics sounds can echo round the room, or sounds may be muffled and quiet. This confuses blind people who need to hear clear sounds to work out where things are.

adapted Changed or improved for a special reason.

AIDS This stands for acquired immune deficiency syndrome. AIDS destroys white blood cells in the body so the body cannot protect itself against diseases. Some diseases affect the eyes.

bionic Something that has had a natural part replaced with electronic equipment.

Braille A system of writing invented by a Frenchman called Louis Braille. Each letter is made up of a simple pattern of raised dots. Blind people read each letter by touching it. Some blind people don't read Braille because their sense of touch is not good enough.

cane A long white stick that blind people often use to guide them around obstacles or let other people know they are blind. There are three kinds of canes. They are all white and they can be folded up when they are not being used. The safest and most useful cane is called the long cane.

cataracts A cataract is a clouding of the lens. Some cataracts are so bad that the person can hardly see at all. An operation can break up the cataract and wash it out of the eye. Doctors can also replace the damaged lens with a special plastic lens.

contrasting When two colours are contrasting they are very different from each other, so each colour stands out clearly. Yellow and black are contrasting colours, but yellow and white are not.

diabetes A disease that stops the body controlling the level of sugar in the blood. This causes problems such as tiredness, thirstiness and blurred vision. People with diabetes must have treatment or their eyesight could be permanently damaged.

echo A sound that bounces back. Echoes are loudest in a building or a tunnel. If you walk along a quiet corridor at school you will hear the echo of your footsteps. Blind people listen to echoes all the time. This helps them to work out where they are.

gadget A small mechanical device or piece of equipment.

German measles A disease also called rubella. It causes a sore throat and a skin rash. In the past many children were born blind and deaf because their mothers had German measles when they were pregnant. Nowadays all girls are given a vaccination (injection) to protect them against this disease. Some people like Helen Keller had German measles when they were young, and it affected their sight and hearing.

glaucoma A type of eye disease caused by watery liquid inside the eye pressing too hard against the nerve and damaging it. This can cause the person to lose some sight or even become blind.

guide dog A dog trained to lead a blind person around. Guide dogs can be very helpful. Not all blind people want a guide dog, and some people are too young or too old to look after a dog properly.

laser A laser is a very thin and powerful beam of light. The light does not spread out like the light from a lamp or a torch, so it can be directed exactly on to a certain point. Lasers can also be used in equipment that warns people of obstacles ahead. The laser bounces off objects and sends a signal to the blind person.

lens The clear part of the eye that we see though. Images are then directed on to the retina.

long-sighted People who are long-sighted find it hard to see objects close to them.

magnifier A lens that you look through to see a larger image of something. Magnifiers are useful to partially-sighted people for reading or doing something fiddly like sewing on a button. Some magnifiers stand on the table and others hang round the person's neck.

nerve A nerve is a tiny, thin thread that carries messages to your brain. There are nerves in all parts of our bodies.

partially-sighted People who are partially-sighted have some vision but it is not very clear. They can see more than people we call blind.

programmed Specially designed to do a certain thing. Talking bus stops of the future will be specially programmed by computer to read out timetables and announce when a bus has arrived.

radar A piece of equipment that picks up signals from objects and makes a sound. The blind person then knows that they must avoid the obstacle ahead. Some radar equipment is not very useful because it only detects nearby objects and does not pick up signals from obstacles such as steps. Radar devices can be very expensive.

retina The retina is the back of the eye. It is very sensitive to light. Images of what you see are carried from the retina to the brain. The brain then recognizes the images.

short-sighted People who are short-sighted can see well close-up but find it difficult to see things that are far away. Short-sightedness is very common, and it often becomes worse as people grow older.

tactile Something that can be touched.

transmit To send or pass on.

Index